LOVE

Alexander Zeldin has formed an ensemble of actors in the
UK with the aim of collaborating together long term in
projects where he writes through a devising process. Their
projects include *Doing the Idiots* (National Theatre Studio,
2012 – a response to Lars von Trier's film *The Idiots*), *Shemehe*
and *Beyond Caring* (Yard Theatre, 2014 and National
Theatre, 2015). Zeldin's work has been recognised by a
nomination for the Rolex Mentor Protégé Award in 2012,
for the leading young artistic voices of the future. He is a
recipient of the Quercus Trust Award 2015 and has been
appointed Associate Director at Birmingham Repertory
Theatre.

Alexander Zeldin

LOVE

Second Edition

Bloomsbury Methuen Drama
An imprint of Bloomsbury Publishing Plc

B L O O M S B U R Y
LONDON • OXFORD • NEW YORK • NEW DELHI • SYDNEY

The script has changed since rehearsals.

Bloomsbury Methuen Drama

An imprint of Bloomsbury Publishing Plc

Imprint previously known as Methuen Drama

50 Bedford Square	1385 Broadway
London	New York
WC1B 3DP	NY 10018
UK	USA

www.bloomsbury.com

**BLOOMSBURY, METHUEN DRAMA and the
Diana logo are trademarks of Bloomsbury Publishing Plc**

First published 2016

This edition, with changes to the script, published 2017

© Alexander Zeldin, 2016, 2017

British Library Cataloguing-in-Publication Data
A catalogue record for this book is available from the British Library.

ISBN: PB: 978-1-3500-4143-1
ePDF: 978-1-3500-4144-8
ePub: 978-1-3500-4145-5

Library of Congress Cataloging-in-Publication Data
A catalog record for this book is available from the Library of Congress

Cover design: Adriana Brioso

Typeset by Mark Heslington Ltd, Scarborough, North Yorkshire

To find out more about our authors and books visit *www.bloomsbury.com*.
Here you will find extracts, author interviews, details of forthcoming
events and the option to sign up for our *newsletters*.

'Zeldin creates engrossing drama out of the daily rituals of survival . . . But, while [he] shows rather than tells, he makes the point that these people have done nothing wrong: they are simply victims of a dearth of social housing and arbitrary caps to the benefit system. They are also made to suffer needlessly . . . But Zeldin's particular achievement is to show people's capacity for endurance. Tempers may flare and tensions rise, but his play is both about the dignity and the love that survive even in the harshest circumstances.' *Guardian*

'It's deliberately untheatrical and yet perfectly suited to theatre, where we sit and wait with a character for the kettle to boil. Just as in his earlier work *Beyond Caring*, Zeldin uses silence potently: often not much happens because that is the nature of being in limbo.' *Financial Times*

'I should stress that *Love* is neither tub-thumping agit-prop, nor class tourism. Whatever Zeldin's political purpose, he keeps his opinions firmly in the background and, instead, focuses on the personal plight of several individuals, which leaves you wanting to know much, much more about how they ended up spending the festive season in such horribly reduced circumstances . . . Zeldin's devised play slowly builds up a picture of his characters through details which, no matter how small, accrue a considerable emotional power . . . It is clear that there is no easy escape for the characters in *Love*, and no easy answers for anyone who dares to see this quietly provocative, necessary play.' *Daily Telegraph*

'Zeldin doesn't just push emotional buttons, he dons great big boots and jumps on them from a height; even before the rather extraordinary gesture that takes place towards the end, people are weeping. But we should weep . . . This feels designed to make you angry. It wants you to look – and then it asks you to act.' *Stage*

Birmingham Repertory Theatre and
the National Theatre present

LOVE

By Alexander Zeldin

LOVE received its world premiere in the Dorfman Theatre
at the National Theatre, London on 13 December 2016
and opened in The STUDIO at Birmingham Repertory
Theatre on 26 January 2017.

CAST

Tharwa	**Hind Swareldahab**
Colin	**Nick Holder**
Dean	**Luke Clarke**
Paige	**Emily Beacock**
	Darcey Brown
	Grace Doherty
Barbara	**Anna Calder-Marshall**
Emma	**Janet Etuk**
Jason	**Vitaly Outkine**
	Yonatan Pelé Roodner
	Bobby Stallwood
Adnan	**Ammar Haj Ahmad**

CREATIVES

Director	**Alexander Zeldin**
Designer	**Natasha Jenkins**
Lighting Designer	**Marc Williams**
Sound Designer	**Josh Anio Grigg**
Movement	**Marcin Rudy**
Fight Director	**Kev McCurdy**
Company Voice Work	**Cathleen McCarron**
Staff Director	**Diyan Zora**
Company Stage Manager	**Ruth Morgan**
Deputy Stage Manager	**Jo Nield**
Assistant Stage Manager	**Hannan Finnegan**
Chaperones	**Frank Ravenscroft and Denise Smith**
Dresser	**Tracey Dolby**

Alexander Zeldin, Associate Director of Birmingham Repertory Theatre, is supported by the Quercus Trust

Cast Biographies

Emily Beacock   Paige

Emily Beacock trains at New London Performing Arts Centre, West End MT and Chickenshed.

Theatre credits include: *Bugsy Malone* (Lyric Hammersmith); *The Night Before Christmas*, *Sleeping Beauty* and *The Twelve Days of Christmas* (Chickenshed); and *Once the Musical* (Phoenix).

Television credits include: *The Secret Life of Twins* (ITV).

Film credits include: *Ready Player One* (Amblin Entertainment) and *Our Kind of Traitor* (Potboiler Productions).

Darcey Brown   Paige

Theatre credits include: *The Railway Children* (King's Cross).

Film credits include: *Denial* (Denial Ltd) and *What Happened to Monday?* (RDL Productions).

Anna Calder-Marshall   Barbara

Anna Calder-Marshall trained at LAMDA and was awarded the Ellen Terry Scholarship.

Theatre credits include: *Evening at the Talk House*, *The Secret Rapture* and *The Seagull* (National Theatre); *The Philistines* (Royal Shakespeare Company); *Temple* and *Lie of the Mind* (Donmar); *The Herd* (Bush Theatre); *Salt, Root and Roe* (Trafalgar Studios); *Open Court: Death Tax, In the Republic of Happiness* and *Uncle Vanya* (Royal Court); *Pastoral* (Soho/HighTide); *Danger: Memory!: I Can't Remember Anything* (Jermyn Street); *The House of Bernarda Alba* and *Love – The Musical* (Lyric Hammersmith); *The Bargain* and *Troilus and Cressida* (Bath Theatre Royal); *A Kind of Alaska* and *Tejas Verdes* (Gate); *Comfort Me with Apples*, *Dear Janet Rosenberg*, *Dear Mr Kooning* and *Formation Dancers* (Hampstead); *The Importance of Being Earnest* (Oxford Playhouse); *Bird Calls* and *The Birthday Party* (Sheffield Crucible); *Antigone* (Old Vic); *Measure For Measure, The Devil Is An Ass, Romeo and Juliet, Saint Joan, Peer Gynt* and *A Severed Head* (Birmingham Repertory Theatre); *The Lady's Not for Burning* and

Caesar and Cleopatra (Chichester); *Major Barbara*, *Twelfth Night* and *The Wild Duck* (Lyceum); *Humble Boy* (Gielgud); and *Absurd Person Singular* (Criterion).

Television credits include: *Casualty*, *Holby Blue*, *Dalziel and Pascoe*, *Doctor Who*, *Lovejoy*, *Titus Andronicus*, *Strangers and Brothers*, *The Winter's Tale*, *Bloomers*, *Matilda's England*, *A Woman's Place?*, *The Duchess of Duke Street*, *Under Western Skies*, *Play for Today*, *The Wednesday Play* and *The Raging Moon* (BBC); *Scott and Bailey* (Red Productions); *13 Steps Down* (Ardmore Studios); *New Tricks* (Wall to Wall); *The Bill* (Talkback Thames); *Poirot* (Carnival Films); *Midsomer Murders* (Bentley Productions); *Witness Against Hitler* (The Drama House); *Casebook of Sherlock Holmes*, *King Lear*, *Crown Court*, (Granada Television); *Heartbeat* (Yorkshire Television); *Blood Royal: William the Conqueror* (British Lion Films); *Rules of Engagement* (Futuremedia); *Inspector Morse* (Zenith Entertainment); *Hammer House of Horror* (Chips Productions); *Affairs of the Heart* (London Weekend Television); *Male of the Species* (Independent Television – Emmy Award for Outstanding Single Performance by an Actress in a Supporting Role); *Sanctuary* (Associated-Rediffusion Television); and *Love Story* (Associated Television).

Film credits include: *Anna Karenina* (Icon); *Saint-Ex* (BBC); *Zulu Dawn* (Zulu Dawn NV); and *Wuthering Heights* (American International Pictures).

Recent radio credits include: *Eugenie Grandet* with Ian McKellen and *Subterranean Homesick Blues* with Bill Nighy.

Luke Clarke   Dean

Luke Clarke trained on the Acting and Contemporary Theatre course at East 15.

Theatre credits include: *Beyond Caring* (National Theatre/The Yard); *Marguerite* (Sadler's Wells); *Doing the Idiots* (National Theatre Studio); and *Touch Me* (Rustaveli, Tbilisi).

He is also co-founder and Artistic Director of The Alchemist Theatre Company.

www.thealchemisttheatre.co.uk

Grace Doherty   Paige

Grace Doherty trained at Theatre Studio West.

Theatre credits include: *X* (Royal Court) and *Made in Dagenham* (Adelphi).

Television credits include: *Casualty* (BBC).

Short-film credits include: *Eleanor* (NFTS).

Radio credits include: *Home Front* (BBC Radio 4).

Janet Etuk   Emma

Janet Etuk trained on the Acting and Contemporary Theatre course at East 15.

Theatre credits include: *Beyond Caring* (National Theatre/The Yard); *The Love I Feel Is Red* (Tobacco Factory/Òran Mór); *The Spanish Tragedy* (Old Red Lion); Alchemist's *Dead Grass* and *Sealand* (Arcola); Unstable Table's *Lone Rangers* (Blue Elephant); *The Story of the Four-Minute Mile* (Oxford Playhouse); *Doing the Idiots* (National Theatre Studio); and *Touch Me* (Rustaveli, Tbilisi).

Short-film credits include: *Expecting* (Cestoda Productions).

Ammar Haj Ahmad   Adnan

Ammar Haj Ahmad trained at the Higher Institute for Dramatic Arts, Damascus.

Theatre credits include: *The Great Survey of Hastings* and *Babel* (WildWorks); *Kan Yama Kan* (Cockpit); *Mawlana* (Mosaic Rooms); *The Knight and the Crescent Hare* (Ankur Productions); *One Thousand and one Nights* (Dash Arts); and *Historie d'Amour* (French Cultural Exchange).

Television credits include: *Agatha Raisin* (Free @ Last TV) and *Letters from Baghdad* (Between The Rivers Productions) and many Syrian series.

Film credits include: *Wall* (National Film Board of Canada); *Round Trip* (Bizibi); *Maqha Almawt* (Points Production); *Wada'an* (National

Cinema Corp) and *Monologue* (SNCC); and the short films *London Tomorrow, Alegna* and *The Logic of Birds*.

Nick Holder   Colin

Theatre credits include: *The Threepenny Opera, An Oak Tree, Everyman, 50 Years on Stage, London Road* (original and revival cast), *South Pacific, Sweeney Todd, The Resistible Rise of Arturo Ui, The Miser* and *The Wind in the Willows* (National Theatre); *The Winter's Tale, The Merry Wives of Windsor, The Taming of the Shrew, Antony and Cleopatra, The Beggar's Opera* and *As You Like It* (Royal Shakespeare Company); *Into the Woods* (Donmar); *Richard III* and *The Music Man* (Regent's Park); *Little Fish* and *A Day at the Racists* (Finborough); *Assassins* (Union); and *The 39 Steps, The Drowsy Chaperone, Jesus Christ Superstar, Les Misérables* and *Miss Saigon* (West End).

Television credits include: *Siblings* (Bwark Productions); *WPC 56* and *Coalition* (Cuba Pictures/Channel 4); *The Game, By Any Means, Some Girls, Way to Go, Holby City, Psychoville, Born and Bred, 'Orrible, EastEnders* and *The Fast Show* (BBC); *Peaky Blinders* (Tiger Aspect); *The Job Lot* (Big Talk Productions); *Parade's End* (HBO/BBC); *Planespotting* (Granada Television); and *London's Burning* (London Weekend Television).

Film credits include: *London Road* and *Broken* (Cuba Pictures); *The World's End* (Working Title); *Les Misérables* (Working Title/Universal Films); *Anna Karenina* (Green Twig Films); *Clubbed* (Formosa Films); *Lady Godiva: Back in the Saddle* (Godiva Productions); *Sex Lives of Potato Men* (Devotion Films); *Four Feathers* (Miramax Films); *The Final Curtain* (Young Crossbow); *The Criminal* (Palm Pictures); and *Evita* (Wondervale Limited).

Vitaly Outkine   Jason

Vitaly Outkine has trained with The Young Actors Theatre Islington, Stagecoach, Sylvia Young and Greenwich and Lewisham Young People's Theatre.

LOVE is his professional theatre debut, and he has appeared in a music video for the group Itchy Teeth.

Yonatan Pelé Roodner   Jason

LOVE is Yonatan Pelé Roodner's professional theatre debut.

Bobby Stallwood   Jason

Theatre credits include: *The Wizard of Oz* and *Treasure Island* (Act II) and *Macbeth* and *Romeo and Juliet* (Shakespeare Schools Festival).

Hind Swareldahab   Tharwa

LOVE is Hind Swareldahab's professional theatre debut.

Creative Biographies

Alexander Zeldin   Writer and Director

Alexander Zeldin has worked across the world as a theatre-maker and director. His projects include directing at the Mariinsky Opera and the Naples Festival (European Theatre Company 2010), and *Macbeth* in South Korea (Korean Critics' Choice, 2011) and *Black Battles with Dogs* (Southwark Playhouse, 2012). In 2013 he assisted Peter Brook and Marie-Hélène Estienne on *A Magic Flute* at the CICT?Théâtre des Bouffes du Nord. In 2011, he formed an ensemble of actors in the UK with the aim of collaborating on long-term projects, which he writes. Past plays include *Doing the Idiots* (National Theatre Studio, 2012) and *Shemehe* (Rustaveli Theatre, Georgia). His last play, *Beyond Caring*, premiered at The Yard Theatre before transferring to the National Theatre's Temporary Theatre in 2015. He is a current recipient of the Quercus Award, and Associate Director at Birmingham Repertory Theatre until 2017.

Natasha Jenkins   Designer

Natasha Jenkins studied Theatre, Film and Television at the University of Glasgow.

Her previous work as a designer includes: *Beyond Caring* (National Theatre's Temporary Theatre); *20b* (Birmingham Repertory Theatre); *Beyond Caring* (European tour/The Yard); *How Was It for You?* (Unicorn); *Glengarry Glen Ross* (Gilmorehill Theatre G12); and the short films *Loose Ends*, *Latitude Project* and *Here We Are*.

She was design assistant on *The Velveteen Rabbit* (Unicorn) and *The Events* (ATC). Work as a director includes *1001 Nights* (Queen's, Hornchurch/tour) and a rehearsed reading of *Christmas Is Miles Away* (Unicorn).

As assistant director, her work includes: *Tonight at 8.30* (Nuffield/ English Touring Theatre); *Liar Liar* (Unicorn); *The Only True History of Lizzie Finn* (Southwark Playhouse); *1001 Nights* (Unicorn/ Transport); and *Table* (National Theatre Studio).

Work as a dramaturg includes: *No Weddings nor a Funeral* (RADA Festival) and *20b* (Birmingham Repertory Theatre). She has previously worked as a stage manager at the National Theatre, the

Young Vic, the Almeida, the Royal Court, the Unicorn, Tramway and in the West End.

Marc Williams   Lighting Designer

Marc Williams trained at the Liverpool Institute for Performing Arts. He is currently the Lighting Operations Manager for the National Theatre.

Design work for the National Theatre includes: *Beyond Caring*, and he was associate on *Mother Courage and Her Children*, *Hamlet* and *Fela!*.

Other theatre work includes: *Home* (Unity); *Beyond Caring* (The Yard); *Black Battles with Dogs* (Southwark Playhouse); *Blackberry Trout Face* (tour for 20 Stories High); *The Dreadful Hours* (tour); *Endz* and *Cruel Sea* (Liverpool Everyman and Playhouse); and *Wild Animus* (International Tour for Void Projects).

Josh Anio Grigg   Sound Designer

Josh Anio Grigg is a producer, sound designer and artist from London. He completed a Drama, Theatre and Performance degree at Roehampton University of Surrey in 2008. He has designed sound for many spaces across London as well as creating and performing music at festivals across Europe.

Marcin Rudy   Movement

Marcin Rudy is a movement director, actor and teacher. Between 2000 and 2012 he collaborated with Song of the Goat Theatre as a performer/deviser. After leaving the company he focused on creating training for actors with special emphasis on the physical-emotional connection. He has collaborated with Alexander Zeldin on many shows, including *Romeo and Juliet* (Teatro Mercadante, Naples); *Doing the Idiots* (National Theatre Studio); and *Black Battles with Dogs* (Southwark Playhouse).

Kev McCurdy   Fight Director

Kev McCurdy is an Equity professional fight director. He trained as an actor at Royal Welsh College of Music and Drama from 1988 to

1991 and assisted the fight master during that period, gaining combat teacher status in 1993 and Equity professional fight director's status in 1996. He has been Royal Welsh College's resident fight master since 2005 and has worked on a variety of stage, TV, film and music-video projects around the UK and abroad.

His work includes: *The Suicide, The Motherfucker with the Hat, The Beaux' Stratagem* and *13* (National); *The Heart of Robin Hood* (also Norway and Sweden); *Marat/Sade, Julius Caesar, Much Ado About Nothing, The Jew of Malta, Love's Labour's Lost* and *Othello* (Royal Shakespeare Company); *To Kill a Mockingbird* and *Mogadishu* (Royal Exchange/Lyric Hammersmith/UK tour); *A View from the Bridge* (UK tour); *Batman Live* (world arena tour); *Troilus and Cressida* and *The Last Days of Troy* (Royal Exchange/Shakespeare's Globe); *Romeo and Juliet* and *King Lear* (UK/Middle East tour); *The Taming of the Shrew* (on tour in UK and Europe); *The Lightning Child* (world premiere), *Julius Caesar, The Changeling, The Frontline* (world premiere), *The Duchess of Malfi, Bedlam, The Malcontent* and *The Comedy of Errors* (Shakespeare's Globe); *The House that Will Not Stand, Broken Glass* and *Multitudes* (Tricycle); and *Miss Saigon* (world premiere) and *Sweeney Todd* (UK premiere) in London's West End.

Television and film credits include: *John Carter of Mars* (Walt Disney Pictures); *Season of the Witch* (Atlas Entertainment); *Hunky Dory* (Film Agency for Wales); S*et Fire to the Stars* (Mad as Birds); *Canaries* (Maple Dragon Films); *Stella* (Tidy Productions); and *Hinterland* (A113Media International).

Cathleen McCarron   Company Voice Work

Cathleen McCarron is Assistant Voice Coach at the National Theatre and also works with the MA Acting (Classical and Contemporary) students at the Royal Central School of Speech and Drama.

Previous voice coaching work includes: *A Pacifist's Guide to the War on Cancer, The Threepenny Opera, Les Blancs, Ma Rainey's Black Bottom, Pomona* and *The Comedy of Errors* (National); *People, Places and Things* (Wyndham's); *Julius Caesar, Much Ado About Nothing, Matilda* and *Song of Songs* (Royal Shakespeare Company); *Diary of a Madman* (Gate); *Namatjira* (Southbank Centre); *The Glass Supper*

(Hampstead); *Tape* (Trafalgar Studios); *Jack and the Beanstalk* (Liverpool Everyman); and *Othello* (Bussey Building, Peckham).

She has also worked extensively with non-performers on voice and communication skills and her clients have included scientists for the United Nations, lawyers, teachers, journalists, politicians and make-up artists, amongst many others.

She originally trained in acting at the Royal Conservatoire of Scotland and has worked across film, theatre, stage, television and voiceover for several years. She trained in voice/dialect coaching at the Royal Central School of Speech and Drama, graduating with distinction, and worked at the Royal Shakespeare Company and at several accredited drama schools before joining the National Theatre.

Diyan Zora   Staff Director

Diyan Zora was previously staff director for *Evening at the Talk House* at the National Theatre. She was associate director for *My Name Is*, which toured the UK.

Assistant-director work includes: *Fireworks* and *Wolf from the Door* (Royal Court) and *The Nightmares of Carlos Fuentes* (Arcola).

As a director, work includes: *Advice to Iraqi Women* (Unity Liverpool and the Old Red Lion); *Gather Ye Rosebuds* (Theatre503/Nightingale, Brighton – winner of Best New Play at the Brighton Fringe); *Twelfth Night* (The Cockpit); and *Othello* (Baron's Court).

She graduated with a BA in Law and English Literature from Nottingham University, a diploma in Communist Studies from Karlova University, Prague and a master's in Human Rights from SOAS, London.

About Birmingham Repertory Theatre

Birmingham Repertory Theatre Company is one of Britain's leading producing theatre companies. Founded in 1913 by Sir Barry Jackson, Birmingham Repertory Theatre Company rapidly became one of the most famous and exciting theatre companies in the country, launching the careers of many great British actors including Laurence Olivier, Ralph Richardson, Edith Evans, Paul Scofield, Derek Jacobi, Elizabeth Spriggs and Albert Finney.

The REP's mission is to inspire a lifelong love of theatre in the diverse communities of Birmingham and beyond. As well as presenting over 60 productions on its three stages every year, the theatre tours its productions nationally and internationally, showcasing theatre made in Birmingham.

The commissioning and production of new work lies at the core of The REP's programme and over the last 15 years, the company has produced more than 130 new plays. The theatre's outreach programme engages with over 7,000 young people and adults through its learning and participation programme, equating to 30,000 individual educational sessions. The REP is also committed to nurturing new talent through its youth theatre groups and training for up and coming writers, directors and artists through its REP Foundry initiative.

Many of The REP's productions go on to have lives beyond Birmingham, transferring to the West End and touring nationally and internationally. Recent transfers and tours include *The Government Inspector* (2016 UK tour), *Of Mice and Men* (2016 UK tour), *Anita and Me* (Theatre Royal Stratford East), *Back Down* (UK tour), *The King's Speech* (national tour), *Rudy's Rare Records* (Hackney Empire), *Khandan (Family)* (Royal Court), *Twelve Angry Men* (West End), Philip Pullman's *I Was a Rat!* (national tour) and Kate Tempest's *Hopelessly Devoted* (national tour).

The REP's long-running production of *The Snowman* celebrated its 21st anniversary in 2014. It has become a must-see fixture in London's West End calendar, playing to packed houses at the Peacock Theatre every Christmas for a record-breaking 18 years. *The Snowman* also tours regularly across the UK and to theatres in Holland, Korea, Japan and Finland. The REP has recently won the Best New Play award at the UK Theatre Awards 2016, for *Cuttin' It*, a Young Vic/Royal Court Theatre co-production with The REP, Sheffield Theatres and The Yard Theatre. It also won five awards at The Drum Dream Awards, recognising the best creative marketing, digital and social strategies in the UK, for 'we're here because we're here' – a UK-wide event with thousands of volunteers to mark the centenary of the Battle of the Somme, which was produced by The REP and the National Theatre in July 2016. The REP was also named Venue of the Year at the Birmingham Awards.

Artistic Director **Roxana Silbert**

Executive Director **Stuart Rogers**

birmingham-rep.co.uk

Box Office: **0121 236 4455**

Administration: **0121 245 2000**

About the National Theatre

The National Theatre, where this play had its premiere in 2016, makes world-class theatre that is entertaining, challenging and inspiring. And we make it for everyone.

We stage up to 30 productions at our South Bank home each year, ranging from reimagined classics – such as Greek tragedy and Shakespeare – to modern masterpieces and new work by contemporary writers and theatre-makers. The work we make strives to be as open, as diverse, as collaborative and as national as possible. Much of that new work is researched and developed at the NT Studio: we are committed to nurturing innovative work from new writers, directors, creative artists and performers. Equally, we are committed to education, with a wide-ranging Learning programme for all ages in our new Clore Learning Centre and in schools and communities across the UK.

The National's work is also seen on tour throughout the UK and internationally, and in collaborations and co-productions with regional theatres. Popular shows transfer to the West End and occasionally to Broadway; and through the National Theatre Live programme, we broadcast live performances to 2,000 cinemas in 50 countries around the world. Through *National Theatre: On Demand. In Schools*, acclaimed, curriculum-linked productions are free to stream on demand in every primary and secondary school in the country. Online, the NT offers a rich variety of innovative digital content on every aspect of theatre.

We do all we can to keep ticket prices affordable and to reach a wide audience, and use our public funding to maintain artistic risk-taking, accessibility and diversity.

Chair of NT Board **Sir Damon Buffini**

Deputy Chair **Kate Mosse**

Director of the National Theatre **Rufus Norris**

Executive Director **Lisa Burger**

Box office and information +44 (0) 20 7452 3000

National Theatre, Upper Ground,
London SE1 9PX

nationaltheatre.org.uk

Registered Charity No: 224223

Registered as a company limited by guarantee in England: 749504

Birmingham Repertory Theatre Staff

Aimee Sheriff
Jess Vantielcke
Lauren Young

Theatre Sales Manager
Gerard Swift

Assistant Theatre & Sales Managers
James Dakers
Rachel Foster
Kieran Johnson
Maria Kavalieros

Theatre & Sales Assistants
Jess Clixby
Rachel Cooper
Robert Flynn
Hannah Kelly
Sebastian Maynard-Francis
Eileen Minnock
Carla Smith
Rhys Worgan

Theatre Assistants
Daniel Carter
Caitlin Edwards
Philip Evans
Anne Farley
Claire Healy
Kirsty Holmes
Elli Katsaouni
Imaani Philips
Liz Wormald

Customer Service Apprentices
Imaani Philips
Sharaye Wright

Theatre Operations Manager
Nigel Cairns

Theatre Concierge
Davine Brown
Andrew Daniels

Theatre Housekeeper
Jane Browning

Theatre Cleaning Assistants
Sandra Bailey
Neville Claxton
Debra Cuthill
Ilyas Fareed
Tracey O'Dell
Ade Ogunbase
Oscar Sagra
Beverley Shale

Head of Production
Tomas Wright

Production Manager
Milorad Žakula

Company Manager
Ruth Morgan

Head of Wardrobe
Kay Wilton

Cutter/Maker
Sue Nightingale

Wardrobe Assistant
Julie Pountney

Head of Lighting
Andrew Fidgeon

Senior Technician (Lighting)
Simon Bond

Technician (Lighting)
Alex Boucher
Dermot Finnegan
Max Sherwin-Jones

Head of Sound & AV
Dan Hoole

Senior Technician (Sound & AV)
Clive Meldrum

Technician (Sound)
Andy Gregory

Head Scenic Artist
Christopher Tait

Head of Technical Design
Ebrahim Nazier

Head of Construction
Margaret Rees

Senior Scenic Maker
Neil Parkes

Scenic Maker
Ed Cartwright

Technical Co-ordinator
Adrian Bradley

Technical Events Manager
Chris Ball

Senior Technician (Stages)
Ross Gallagher

Technician (Stages)
Oscar Turner

Building Maintenance Technician
Leon Gatenby

With thanks to all our Casual Staff and Volunteers

National Theatre *Love* Production Staff

Project Producer	Fran Miller
Production Manager	Emily Seekings
Casting	Charlotte Bevan and Jacob Sparrow
Stage Manager	Jane Suffling
Deputy Stage Manager	Jo Nield
Assistant Stage Manager	Ian Farmery
Project Draughting	Emma Pile and Daniel Radley-Bennet
Digital Art	Daniel Radley-Bennet
Costume Supervisor	Lydia Crimp
Wigs, Hair & Make-up Supervisor	Adele Brandman
Prop Supervisor	Eleanor Smith
Prop Buyer	Sian Willis
Lighting Supervisor	Michael Harpur
Lighting Programmer	Daniel Murfin
Sound & Video Supervisor	Sarah Weltman
Stage Supervisor	Shane Hover
Rigging Supervisors	Barry Peavot and David Borrell
Construction Supervisor	David Cotton
Scenic Art Supervisor	Ian Cooper
NT Design Assistant	Jacob Hughes
Design Assistants	Jemima Robinson and Nate Gibson
Production Photographer	Sarah Lee

I would like to thank Louise Walker, Renée and all her family. Esther, Verna, Renata, Possy, Aso as well as all those who spent time with me and the team. Write for Life, Shelter, Z2K, Crisis. Bill Rashleigh, who set this all off, Natasha Jenkins, Josh Grigg, Marc Williams, Diyan Zora, Marcin Rudy, Cathleen McCarron, Kev McCurdy, Emily Seekings, Fran Miller, Jane Suffling, Jo Nield, Ian Farmery, Nyasha Gudo.

Rufus Norris, Ben Power, Dominic Cooke, Roxana Silbert, thank you for your wisdom, support and friendship and for pushing me forward. Emily McLaughlin and all the team at the New Work Department at the National Theatre, where this play was developed, nurtured and loved, Stuart Rogers, Tessa Walker and the whole arts team at The REP, Peter Brook and Marie-Hélène Estienne, Margaret Zeldin, Finbar Williams.

Alexander Zeldin

LOVE

Characters

Dean, *thirty-one, a father, looking for work*

Emma, *twenty-seven, his partner, studying to be a massage and wellness therapist, stepmother to the children and pregnant*

Paige, *eight, his daughter*

Jason, *twelve, his son*

Colin, *fifty, a man who is a carer to his mother.*

Barbara, *his mother*

Tharwa, *fortyish, a mother without her children*

Adnan, *thirty-fiveish, a man who is injured*

Notes

/ is an interruption

'.' is a thought that doesn't become a word

Act One

Scene One

6.30 a.m.

Lights come up on the common room of a temporary housing facility. There is a kitchen area with dishes piled up, some tables and chairs. At the top end of the room there are a couple of doorways, through which, when opened, we can glimpse two very cramped bedrooms. Downstage, there is a toilet, the door of which has been left open and the light on. The room itself is quite dark; it has a feeling of being inhospitable, cold. The only thing sifting through is an overcast December light from the skylight in the roof. There is a tree above the roof that intermittently brushes against the skylight.

The audience are sat around in such a way that the actors can move freely amongst them.

After a time, a woman comes through, **Tharwa***. She goes to the kitchen with a plastic bag full of food. She makes some toast and puts the kettle on to boil.*

A short time as she waits. She is half turned towards us.

A door upstage opens. **Colin** *comes out in his pants. He hesitates, but crosses the stage to the toilet.*

Tharwa *decides to go back to her room.*

During the above there have been faint noises from the other room: the sound of an alarm clock, children's voices rising above the sound of adults. **Dean** *has woken up* **Jason** *and asked him to get dressed.*

The door of the other room opens. **Dean** *goes to the toilet, with* **Paige***.*

Dean   Wait, love

Paige   I need the loo, Dad, I need the loo

Dean   Wait, wait, I just need to clean it first

Paige   Dad

Dean   Wait there

As he turns to go back to the toilet **Colin** *and* **Barbara** *are setting out.*

He sends **Barbara** *across to the loo; she gets going before* **Paige** *can.*

Colin   You ok

Barbara   Yeh . . .

Dean   You go first

Colin   Cheers, thank you

Paige *waits silently by the wall, then her father brings her closer to the loo.*

Paige   I want the loo I want the loo.

Dean   Ok.

Barbara *leaves the bathroom at last. And shares a look with* **Paige**.

Paige *looks down on the floor.* **Barbara** *goes back to the room.*

Barbara   .

Paige   .

Paige *wants to go in, but* **Dean** *needs to go in first to clean it up.*

Emma *emerges as* **Dean** *is cleaning the toilet and starts removing bottles from the table.*

Dean   You having a wee?

Paige *goes into the bathroom. In the bedroom* **Jason** *turns the iPad on.*

Emma   Dean, can we eat out here?

Dean   Yeh, I'll give it a quick wipe

As **Paige** *emerges:*

Dean   Have you flushed it?

Right, do it then!

Paige *goes back in and flushes the toilet.*

Dean   Right wash your hands

Paige *does and then goes to other side of the room.* **Emma** *cleans as* **Dean** *puts plates out.*

Music seeps in from the bedroom.

Emma   Jase, turn it off please.

Dean   Paige, come and sit down please.

He goes to **Jason** *in the bedroom.*

Dean   Turn it down or turn it off mate yeah

Emma *takes a slice of toast to* **Paige**.

Emma   There you go

Paige   No I want butter

Emma   We don't have any but your dad's going shopping later

Paige   It's disgusting

Emma   It's just jam, Paige

Paige   We always have butter. (*She coughs.*)

Emma   Just eat it please. Eat

Dean *gets butter from another guest's fridge shelf and puts it on* **Paige**'s *toast.*

Emma   What's that?

Paige   I've got a cold

Dean   No you don't.

Emma   Dean?

Dean   It's fine

He goes into the room to give **Jason** *toast. He sits next to* **Jason** *on the bed.*

Paige   I want to go to Sarah's party

Emma   Where is it?

Paige   Airhop

Emma   What's that?

Paige   It's like trampolining but better

Emma   Ok, well, ask your dad

The tree brushes the roof. **Paige** *sits staring at the roof.*

Paige   What's that noise?

Emma   It's just the tree

Jason *crosses the stage with his toothbrush in his mouth.*

Emma   Hey, Jase, you brushing your teeth?

Jason *shows her the toothbrush as if to say 'obviously'.*

He goes into the bathroom. **Dean** *enters.*

Paige   Dad, can I go to Sarah's party?

Dean   What did Emma say?

Paige   She said to ask you

Dean   I'll think about it

D'you remember I'm taking them early today

Emma   Fine

Dean   I'll sort it out, don't worry

Jason *exits the bathroom.*

Jason   The sink's fucked

Dean   Sink's broken.

Jason   Sink's broken and it's fucked

He goes to spit at the sink, very briefly.

This place is crap, Dad

Dean   Just think, it's better that your nan's

Jason   Yeah

Dean   Yeah well we won't be here long, mate

Colin *has come in. He looks into the bedroom, the family look at him.*

Paige   I want cereal

Dean   There isn't any, sorry

Colin   Breakfast

Dean   Yeh. We'll be out of your way in a minute

Colin   Nah nah. You're alright, mate.

A short pause.

I might skip breakfast myself

Had a bit of a sniffy belly recently

Paige   I want cereal.

Colin   You alright, mate, haven't met you yet

Paige   I'm Paige

Colin   I'm Colin, I live next door. (*He goes to shake her hand; she shakes it.*)

Pause.

I had a takeaway last night, I think that did it.

Chinese, yeh fucking guts are a mess, man.

Emma   Sorry are those yours?

Colin   Yeh. Oh sorry yeh.

I'll just put them in the bin, it's fine

He clears away a couple of beer cans that were on the table.

A time. The family eat. Possibly **Colin** *is aware that Barbara will be out any minute.*

Colin   You getting anywhere then

Dean   Sorry?

Colin   Council

Dean   Yeh, we're just waiting on them-on a couple of things /

Colin   Twats aren't they?

Dean   I'm going to sort it out today actually

Paige   I don't want it then

Dean   Fine, don't eat it then

Colin   Yeh I'm actually going to see them next week myself I've you know complained and

.

You working then yeh /

Dean   Yeh

Well I'm trying to find work but it's difficult isn't it

Colin   I'm / sorry . . .? I wasn't working I couldn't, health issues but Yeh I'm developing opportunities at the moment / actually

D'you mind if I have this? (*He takes a bit of toast.*)

Dean   No, it's fine.

Colin   This is all I can fucking handle

Barbara *enters.*

Paige   I want coco pops

Dean   I'm going to pick some stuff up later

Jason   Get some jammy dodgers

Colin   You alright?

Barbara   Yeah.

Nice egg, settle your tum?

1 egg or 2?

Colin   Just 1 yeah.

Emma   Is Sarah you best friend?

Paige   No, I just want to go to her party

Dean   Where is it?

Paige   Near Sarah's

Dean   Ooh, that's a long way

Colin (*to* **Barbara**)   You alright?

Barbara   Yeh

Emma   Dean shall we . . .

Dean   No

Colin (*When he touches plate.*)   Fucking wet.

Barbara *goes to pick up a fork at the sink. She feels unwell and stumbles.*

Colin   Oh come on

Colin *steadies her.*

You alright Mum? I've got you.

Come and sit down, there you go Mum,

Bit too much for you bab, come on lovely

They cross back to table and sit her down.

Dean   Right come on, let's get ready

Dean *and* **Paige** *go into the bedroom.* **Colin** *goes back to the kitchen to try and finish cooking the breakfast.*

Barbara   Sorry, Col

Colin   No, you're alright

Emma *goes to the kitchen and washes up.*

Emma   Sorry. Sorry. Won't be long

Colin   No worries

Emma *goes towards the bedroom as* **Jason** *crosses to the bathroom.*

Colin   They're not yours then the euh . . .?

Emma   No.

She goes into the bedroom.

The branch strokes the roof; the sound is a little like the sound of the sea.

Thinking about the sea, mumbled. **Emma** *goes into the bedroom.*

Barbara (*thinking about the sea, mumbled*)   That sounds a bit like a wave.

Eggy weggy done?

Colin.   Eh? Oh for fuck's sake

It's a bit burnt but I like the dry bits on the bottom you know. It's really nice when you mix them in.

Barbara   Got coleslaw?

Dean *enters with* **Paige**.

Colin   No I'm alright

Emma *enters.*

Dean   See you later, little man. (*He kisses her stomach.*)

It'll be fine yeah?

Emma   Yeah.

Dean, stay calm

Dean *kisses* **Emma**.

Dean   Yeah, I'll call you after. It'll be fine

(*to* **Paige**) Right, come on you.

Jason! Jason.

Jason *runs out of the bathroom.* **Dean**, **Paige** *and* **Jason** *exit.* **Emma** *crosses to the bathroom.*

Colin   No fucking knives

Colin *uses a spatula to put butter on bread then spends a short time noisily emptying the pan of egg on to the bread.*

Barbara   The sooner you get us out of here the better.

He brings breakfast over.

You did talk to them, didn't you?

Colin   Mum, I'm trying to have my fucking breakfast here yeh. I went two days ago, I'm going Monday, I'll even call 'em if you want but you mithering me isn't helping anyone yeh?

Barbara (*with pity*)   When you was a baby you was very quiet Col

Colin   Sorry mum

She goes back into the room.

Pause while **Colin** *eats. He puts his plate by the sink checking that no-one noticed him do it and watches bathroom as* **Emma** *showers.*

Emma *exits wearing a bathrobe and nothing else. –* **Colin** *stops her on the way.*

Colin   You alright

Emma   Yep

Colin   He's off to see them then?

Emma   Yeh / council offices, yeh

Colin   Yeh? / No

Emma   No, we're obviously not counting on being here longer / than a few

Colin   Yeh. Fucking arseholes / aren't they

Emma   you / sorry

Colin   Yeh yeh.

Obviously our situations are different but

Emma   Yeh no of course

Colin   .

That'll help is all I'm saying

Stares at her belly.

You got long to go?

Enter **Barbara**.

Emma   I'm thirty-three weeks /

Colin   Nice

Beat.

Yeh just me and me mum you know

Emma   Right.

Colin   She'd give me the top brick of the chimney / you've only got your own

Barbara   He's my carer.

She gives a chocolate bar to **Colin**.

Colin (*quite slow and softly spoken almost as if it were a confession*)   I'm her carer. Just so you know like, when we agreed to move out of our house we went to look at a home right /

Barbara   But there was a woman tied to a chair /

Colin   They just left them there on the floor in piss and shit

Barbara   And Floyd Mattison

Colin   Twat, that was our person before we're just

Barbara   He said we'd get our own flat cos we agreed to move out

Colin   They just cheat you like we're waiting, fuck, we need somewhere adapted you know our place is like posh flats now /

Emma   Yeh no obviously I don't want – the baby- to be born here /

Colin   No, like obviously yeh but you know they just cheat you.

Emma   Yeah, we were evicted, they put the rent up like overnight and we couldn't afford it /

Colin   You're fucking joking, landlords, vermin, like I'm her carer and you know the council just /don't support you like

Barbara   What's her name?

The little girl

Emma   Paige

Colin   Ah

Barbara   She's a nice little girl.

She begins to walk towards the toilet – embarrassed.

Excuse me

When she gets to the toilet there is a pause, she goes in and then looks out from the loo to **Colin**. *He goes over to the loo.* **Emma** *runs into the room.*

Colin   D'you need anything?

Barbara   No

Colin *is aware that* **Emma** *has gone in. He goes back to his bedroom.*

Tharwa *enters; she is alone on stage. She makes a call to her husband and children, speaking in Arabic.*

Tharwa   Ibrahim? Ibrahim? Are you ok? Hello? Give me Tala

Tala! Tala! Mommy loves you. Tala 'tinkish tinkish'

She makes the gesture of a star with her hands.

Eventually the signal cuts out.

Adnan *arrives. He is carrying a big rucksack and a separate bag. He tentatively, slowly, enters, coming through the audience.*

Adnan   Excuse me? Do you know where room 8 is?

Tharwa   You go through that door there

Adnan   Thank you

He goes to drink water. He wanders upstage.

Here?

Tharwa   Yes.

Here.

Barbara *enters from the bathroom, notices* **Adnan**. *He exits through double doors.*

Tharwa *and* **Barbara** *look at each other.*

Tharwa   Good morning, madam.

Silence. They stand still watching each other.

Blackout.

Scene Two

Later that day, 3 p.m. or so.

Barbara *sitting alone on stage.* **Dean** *enters.*

Simultaneously in the bedroom **Paige** *practises 'Away in a Manger'.*

Dean   Fucking hell

Paige (*singing*)   Away in a manger

Barbara   What?

Jason   Shut up, Paige

Dean   Nothing. Sorry

Enter **Emma**.

Emma   Dean. Did you see the council? You didn't call

Dean (*in movement*)   Yeah. I'm just popping to the toilet

He retreats into the toilet.

Enter **Paige**.

Paige   Dad? Dad, watch me, Dad

Emma   He'll be out in a minute

Paige *puts music track on her phone.*

She rehearses 'Away in a Manger'.

Emma *goes over to* **Paige**.

Emma   Uh . . . not here, babe, do it in the room.

Paige   I can't, Jason's being an idiot and there's no space. I need to practise, I have the nativity

Emma   Yeah well it's too loud

Paige   Leave me alone.

Can you just go. Please

Emma   Well just be quiet then.

After a few moments **Paige** *starts singing along to the track.*

Jason (*from bedroom*)   Shut up, Paige, you can't sing

Emma   Not in here

(*To* **Barbara**.) Sorry

Barbara   It's alright I don't mind

Emma   .

Sorry. She's practising for this Christmas show

Moment of slight connection with **Barbara** *for* **Emma**.

Emma *goes into the bedroom.* **Paige** *continues miming the actions to the song.*

Barbara   What you doing then?

Paige   Stars.

Barbara   I was in a nativity once.

Paige *runs off.*

Barbara   I was a shepherd.

Her feelings are hurt. She goes to her room.

Colin. Colin.

They've been to the council

Emma *is alone onstage.* **Dean** *out of the loo, checking that the coast is clear. We sense that this is already a ritual – to check there is a short moment when there is no one in the space to have dinner.*

Enter **Paige** *from the bedroom. She runs to* **Dean**.

Paige   Dad, Dad, Dad! Jason's being a big bully

Dean   Is he? Your singing sounded lovely

He goes to the kitchen. **Paige** *clings to him.*

Paige   Dad, listen to me. (*Singing.*) Away in a manger

Emma   Dean . . .

Dean   I heard you, it's very good

Paige   Dad, listen, I want to show you my song

Emma   Dean . . .?

Dean   Paige, in a minute

Emma   Paige. I need to talk to your dad.

Paige *runs off.*

Emma   How'd it go?

Dean   It's fine, there's been some sort of mix-up, they've given me a number to call on Monday

Emma   What kind of mix-up?

Dean   There's been crosswires – remember that appointment we missed at the job centre?

Emma   Yeh, on eviction day? But

Dean   I swear it's fine, I was there for eight hours, babe, I'm on it

Kisses her.

(*Picking up the plates.*) I'll put these out

Jason *enters with a football.* **Dean** *puts three plates on the table.*

Emma   Dean . . .

Jason   Dad

He throws the ball to **Dean**.

Dean   What have I told you about playing with that inside

Plays football with the boy. He then goes and has a pillow fight with him in the room.

Jason   Bullshit.

The food is disappointing.

Dean   Come and sit down. Paige, come on. Turn that off please

Emma   Your dad's had a bit of a stressful day, didn't get to the shops, so let's not make a fuss and just eat it yeah?

She sits at the table. **Dean** *brings the rice and serves it onto three plates.*

Dean   Hood off at the table, Jason.

Jason   Is that it?

Dean   Hood off at the table.

He sits at the table.

Paige   Where's your dinner, Dad?

Dean   I've already eaten

Jason   It's not even dinner

Enter **Adnan**. *He looks into the common room and sees it is busy.*

Paige   Who's that?

Emma   He lives upstairs.

Adnan *exits.*

Dean   How was your day?

Emma   Good. I managed to get an appointment on Monday at the hospital. I think I should just check in.

Dean   Great – Jason?

Jason *shrugs his shoulders.*

Dean   Oh that good eh?

(*To* **Paige**.) How about you?

Paige   Good. I got a certificate for being kind

Jason *laughs.*

Dean   Oi

Paige   I got a certificate / for being kind

Jason *laughs in her face.*

Dean   Jason! Go on, who gave you that?

Paige Mrs Watts

Jason Shut up

Paige Dad's asking me, Jason /

Jason I don't care about your certificate –

No one cares

Emma I care

Jason Yeh exactly

Dean Oi!

Paige Shut up, Jason, you're so thick that's why you never get anything at school you're just so stupid

Jason WHAT?

Say that again

Dean Oi!

Jason   SHUT UP, YOU LITTLE BITCH

Paige YOU SHUT UP, JASON

Dean OI THAT'S ENOUGH.

Jason *sits silently for the rest of the meal.*

Silence.

Dean Come on, eat. So?

Paige Nothing, it's just a piece of paper

Emma Still . . .

Paige I don't really need it.

Emma You should be proud of yourself.

Paige Yeah

Dean Well done, love

Pause.

Paige   I'm cold

Dean *gives his jumper to* **Paige**.

Dean   Come on, eat up

Pause. **Emma** *passes her plate to* **Dean**.

Emma   Do you want the rest of this?

Dean   No, you should have it.

Emma   I've had enough

Dean   Thank you

It'll be alright, babe

Colin *enters.*

Colin   Feast. Everyone alright?

Dean   Yeah we're all fine thank you.

Colin   You've got your bidding number then?

Dean   Yeah there's been a mix-up, just a couple of things to sort out / but all fine

Colin   Tell me about it.

Who is your caseworker?

Emma   Angela /

Colin   Harrison? Twat.

Emma   Yeh, do you know her then?

Colin   Yeh we've had her for ages

Emma   How long you been in here?

Colin   About a year, summat like that

Emma   That's not possible though is it they put you here / they're

Colin   It is.

Dean   It's for six weeks maximum by the law that's what they said to us.

Colin   Ha

Emma   It's against the law

Colin   Yeh, love /

Emma   They / we sat in them offices like a week ago, mate, yeh so

Colin   LOVE /

Emma   HANG ON /

Colin   LOVE, I'M NOT BEING FUNNY, BUT THEY CAN DO WHAT THE FUCK THEY WANT

Emma   No, hold on

Colin   LOVE, THE COUNCIL, just cos you're pregnant, yeh, right just cos you're pregnant DOESN'T MEAN YOU CAN'T BE FUCKED, right.

A time. **Emma** *stands and goes towards the bedroom.*

Colin   Sorry. Sorry

Emma   Just because you've been here for that long

Colin   No no

Emma   I mean obviously *your* circumstances are different. I think our situation will change when we / actually get a chance to speak to someone

Colin   Yeh no

Emma   So like if you m /

Dean   Emma

Emma   Yeh it's fine.

Pause. She exits to her room upstage.

Colin *sits downstage in one of the audience-area seats.*

Dean   Do you want to go to the park?

Jason   No

Paige   Yeah

Dean   Go and get your coat then.

Paige *goes into the bedroom then re-enters*

Colin   Sorry / I just

Dean   Yeah, it's fine, just want to get some / air

Colin   Yeh

Dean *and* **Paige** *exit.*

Colin *goes to the family bedroom and listens.*

He knocks on the door.

Colin   Alright

Emma   Yeh /

Colin   Listen no I just wanted to apologise ab / out

Emma   Yeh no look right it's fine it's alright

During the following **Barbara** *enters and then is there overhearing.*

Emma   Thank you for the apology /

Colin   Yeh no /

Emma   But you have to see where I'm coming from. We are trying to stay positive in here, so yeh you've been here for like a year but that doesn't necessarily mean that we are going to be here for a year?

So for you to be bringing that, well, negative energy into the communal area and like you know like when people try to, maybe unintentionally, you know well I

Colin   Yeh

No don't / like / it's bad karma

Pause. They stand in silence.

I'm / sorry, love /

Emma   Yeh no / right /

Colin   Yeh

(*To* **Barbara**.) Y'alright? What?

Barbara   .

Colin   D'you want me to wash your hair?

Barbara   No

Colin   Go on you'll feel better. Just a quick wash

Barbara   No.

Colin   Go on, you always feel happy after.

Barbara   Use the Fairy

Colin   I'm only trying to make you happy

Barbara   Sorry

They cross to the kitchen.

Colin   You lean over

Barbara   Yeh

Colin   Don't get wet as you'll get a cold

He pours and she shrieks.

Barbara   Fucking fuck.

Gone down me neck

Colin   Alright, Mum, I'll put some Fairy on. You've got lovely hair ain't you

Barbara   Gone down me neck

Colin   You're alright, bab.

Barbara   Squeaky

Colin   Squeaky clean

Golden princess

Pause.

Barbara   I love you

Colin   I love you too

Tharwa *enters. Crosses to the bathroom.*

Barbara   Yeah

Get me a towel

Colin.   I'll use this

He takes a tea towel from near the sink.

Barbara   Oh Colin, I need the

Colin   Ok ok

He and **Barbara** *cross to the loo.* **Colin** *bangs on the door.*

Colin   Excuse me! Excuse me!

Can you hurry up please, my mom's

Tharwa   I just come in give me 5 minutes please

Colin   Can't last that long

Sorry it's for my mum.

Tharwa   Don't push the door

Colin   I'm not pushing the door

Mate, hurry up

Cue family argument in bedroom with **Jason** *overheard.*

There are regular interruptions between the two scenes so that in some way they feel like one musical piece. **Colin** *is aware that there are people that could emerge at any moment to this scene.*

Colin (*to* **Tharwa**)   Can you just hold it if you're only having a piss

Tharwa *leaves the bathroom, goes to exit.*

Colin   Thank you, sorry

Emma   Do you think it's ok to talk like that to me to talk like that no it's not

Jason   Shut up

Colin   Do you want some wipes?

Barbara   No

Colin   Are you sure you're going to get it properly clean

Cos I don't want to clean the bed

Barbara   No you're alright

Emma   You can't you're twelve

You haven't got anything in life.

You're not allowed

Jason   I don't give a fuck.

Emma   Yeh go on then /

Jason *walks out.*

Jason *and* **Colin** *look at each other.*

Jason *thinks about running out of the space and then changes his mind – he has nowhere to go but back into the room. He does.*

Colin   Do you want the talcum

Barbara   Nooo

Colin   Y'alright, Mom

Barbara *emerges and they cross slowly to the room.*

Colin   Alright

Love you, Mum

Emma *emerges to study at the table.*

Sorry, love

Adnan *enters, hesitates a beat about going to the sink, apologises and goes back to the room.*

Pause.

Enter **Dean** *and* **Paige** *from the park.*

Dean   It's raining

Emma   Go and get dried off, love

Paige *goes to get dried off in the room. They wait.*

Emma   You alright?

Dean   Yeh I'm alright, you?

Emma   Yeh I'm a bit freaked out by them being there a year . . .

Dean   Yeh but it's not going to be us is it?

Paige *goes into the bedroom.*

Emma   Well what happened then?

Dean   I told you.

Emma   Have you told them everything that's happened to us in the last six weeks ? You've been there /

Dean   I TOLD THEM EVERYTHING – I've been there all day

Emma   I'm not attacking you, Dean.

Dean   You ARE attacking me sorry I'm tired I'm also tired.

Emma   I'm not denying you are tired I just I wasn't there I've been in this room ALL DAY with like, all these people, and it's doing my head in and I just want to check /

Dean   I told you I'VE GOT IT and it's going to be fine you just think about the baby and / stay calm

Emma   I DON'T WANT MY BABY TO BE BORN HERE

Dean   I DON'T WANT MY BABY TO BE BORN HERE
EITHER.

Jason *enters.*

Jason   I want to call Mum

Dean   Well you can't.

Jason   Why?

Emma   Dean!

Dean   Sorry, mate, in a minute yeh

Jason (*under his breath*)   Fucksakes

He goes back into the bedroom.

Dean   I'll call the number on Monday.

Emma   We're low on food

Dean   I'll sort it, I promise

Emma I . . . Love . . .

Emma   No. Please. Sorry.

She takes his phone.

I need to call the council office

Dean   Well the office is closed /

Emma   I need to call them right now /

Dean   There's no point, they've got nothing to do with it,
it's the job centre now so you're just wasting your time

Emma   Go / Go

Dean   You're wasting my minutes as well

He exits to the bedroom.

Emma *tries to make a call.*

Emma   Hi, Angela, my name is Emma Lowell, my partner
Dean Gray came in to see you today. I just wanted to check
in and see if everything is alright cos obviously we filled in all
the paperwork with you and were hopeful to be moving
towards getting a bidding number . . . I just want to make
sure there hasn't been a mix-up because I know you said
you'd be helping us.

Maybe we can have a quick catch-up sometime, I think
you've got all my details, hope you're well, ok, thank you,
bye

Tharwa *enters during the call. She goes to wash a mug in the sink.*

Emma   Excuse me. I think that's our mug

Tharwa   Are you sure?

You're not right

Emma   Sorry I know what my mug looks like

Tharwa   Go and check your stuff. Since you arrived you
looked at me badly. This mug been here for eight months

Emma   I haven't done anything to disrespect you yeh that's
not the way I behave

Tharwa   You looking to me not nice

Emma   Can you listen to me for one minute. I know what
my shit looks like.

Tharwa   I do not like this. I do not like this at all

Emma   Look, it's my stuff.

Can you not touch our stuff cos you don't wash it properly

Tharwa   You are very rude. This is not your mug

I do not like this

They talk over each other. **Tharwa** *exits.*

Emma   Unbelievable

She knocks at her bedroom door.

Dean   Who is it?

Emma   Dean!

She goes in.

Short pause.

Jason *comes out, sits alone at the table.*

Silence.

He starts rapping to himself quietly – he thinks he's alone. He checks it first and then he does a small part of a song by the rapper Baseman.

Enter **Adnan**.

Adnan   Hi

Jason   Hi

They don't know how to communicate. They stop.

Adnan *slowly does a bit of rapping to tease* **Jason**.

Adnan   Yo yo go with the flow.

Jason *is embarassed*

Adnan *exits.*

Jason *alone.*

Blackout.

Act Two

Scene One

Monday morning.

The following scene is a kind of 'ballet' in which the staging carries a lot of the energy.

Actions happen very fast and over the top of each other.

Barbara *is on stage.* **Dean** *is sitting in the audience area on the phone.*

She's looking up at the branch.

Barbara   Fucking stupid cow.

Emma *walks in.* **Barbara** *notices that* **Emma** *is looking at her. She freezes.*

Barbara   .

Emma   .

Babe, Paige needs you to help her in the room

Dean   I'm still on hold

Emma   Well Paige needs you

She goes into the loo. **Dean** *goes into the bedroom.*

Adnan *walks in.* **Barbara** *is scared.*

He puts his stuff in the fridge, moving a few things.

Barbara *thinks about saying something but doesn't.*

Colin *comes in. He's about to go out (he has been threatening to do so all day). He looks at the fridge.*

Barbara   Col . . .

Colin   Scuse me, mate? Scuse me, mate? You alright, mate? You alright? Sorry. You using the middle shelf there? The middle shelf? Yeah, we've had this before with . . . That shelf's ours. Sorry. Can you use the other shelf? No room

Adnan   Sorry.

He moves everything.

Colin   Use the other shelf, use the smaller shelf, is that ok? Is that alright, mate?

Cheers.

(*To* **Barbara**.) You got that letter?

Barbara   Just give me a minute

He goes into the room.

Paige *comes in. Moment of solitude.*

Barbara   Hello

Paige   Hello

Barbara   Are you going to school?

Paige   Yeh

Barbara (*fast*)   I was always so upset at school I don't know why

Paige   .

Barbara   I'm sure you prefer being at school don't you

I wanted to give you something, hang on

Enter **Dean**.

Barbara   I'll get it.

Barbara *exits.*

Emma *enters from the loo. She goes into the bedroom.*

Paige   I'm hungry

Dean   D'you want some toast?

He puts the phone on to loudspeaker and leaves it in the audience seating area on a free chair.

Don't touch that.

Emma *enters with her coat on.*

Emma   Dean, I'm going to the hospital

Dean   I thought you were taking Paige to school

Emma   No I already told you I have to go today. Paige, I'll see you later, have a good day

She exits.

Dean *goes into the bedroom.*

Adnan *goes into the space. He sees* **Paige** *looking lost and kind of dances to the muzak for a second to amuse her.*

She smiles at him. He goes out.

Jason *comes out.*

Dean *re-enters. He makes toast for* **Paige**.

V/O (*on phone*)   Right I can confirm that you have been referred for a sanction due to non-attendance at a job-coaching session.

Dean *picks up the phone.*

Dean   What do you mean you're sanctioning us, what is that?

What, sorry, you can't just cut my money for missing one job-centre appointment on the day I was being evicted. Sorry I said at the time – I was stood in the council building with my children and all our stuff on the day we were being evicted and our caseworker Angela Harrison and she made it clear that this would be passed onto the appropriate people –

But you can't do this to us. My partner is about to have a baby and we need to eat and pay rent. How is this legal? You can't punish us for doing what we were told to do.

I don't want to appeal online! Can I speak to your manager please?

Sorry, no, listen, listen, sorry I wasn't being rude, listen, listen, listen, no, no, sorry

When can I go? That's in forty minutes. Ok, I'll make it, I'll make it

Hangs up. Bangs on the table.

FUCK.

A time. **Paige** *thinks about her options.*

Paige   I want to go to school

Dean   You're not going today

Paige   I want to go to school

Dean   I know you do. I heard you but I haven't got time to take you to school, you'll have to come to the job centre with me

Paige   I want to go

Dean   I just said we aren't going.

Paige *can't deal with it so goes to the toilet to lock herself into it.*

Dean   Paige

Paige

Paige

Come out of the toilet

Paige   No because you keep shouting

Dean   I'm sorry, please come out of the toilet.

Paige, I've got to go

Paige   Fine

Dean   Ok. I'm going to call Emma and tell her to come back for you

Paige   Fine

Dean   Fine

He tries to call **Emma***. Leaves a voicemail.*

Dean   Em, it's me. I'm sorry. You're going to have to come back to the B and B – Paige has locked herself in the toilet. Sorry. Just call me when you get this

(*To* **Jason**.) Right you're going to have to stay and look after your sister

Yes?

Yes?

Jason   Fine

Dean   Right, thank you, mate

I've got to go. Sorry

Paige, stay with your brother, sorry

Paige   Fine

Dean *exits.*

Jason *steps out of the bedroom, but retreats when he sees* **Barbara***.*

Barbara *enters. She looks in her bag.* **Colin** *follows.*

Barbara   Here you are

She gives him a letter.

Colin   Bye, Mum

Barbara   Yeh

Colin   I gotta go now, Mum.

Barbara   Give us a kiss . . .

Col.

He does.

I'm so happy

Colin   Mum, we can't be /

Barbara   No no.

Oh, Col, I hope.

Colin   I'll try my best for us.

I'm going then

Shall I go?

Go on get back in the room

You're being weird.

He exits.

Paige *looks through the door. Goes out . . .*

Barbara   I found the thing I was looking for.

Come here I'll give it to you?

Paige *hesitates and then approaches.*

Barbara *takes a crucifix off her neck and puts it round* **Paige***'s neck.*

Barbara   I feel like a little girl sometimes.

Paige *is trying to get away.* **Barbara** *sort of holds her back, either physically or just by some other means.*

Barbara   Hang on don't go.

Holds her back.

Sorry. Like my body . . . I've got this feeling in my body now like *life is there*! But I can't control my bum you know.

Can you get me a glass of water?

Paige *brings it to her.*

Jason *comes in.*

Jason   Paige

Paige   One second

Barbara   Maybe you can let me talk to you sometimes eh? Yeh? I'm so tired

Jason   Paige, come back to the room

Emma *has rushed back to look after* **Paige**.

Emma (*through the doorway*)   Guys, sorry

Your dad didn't tell me and he just called me now – are you ok?

Paige   Yeh

Emma   So sorry. Thank you

Barbara   We're going soon

Emma   Yeh hopefully / we are too

Barbara   My son's gone to the council

Emma   My partner is / at the

Barbara   He's got a doctor's letter. They promised us a place.

Emma s*miles*.

Emma   Excuse me.

She goes back to her room.

Barbara *waits a moment. She goes back towards her room then pauses outside it. She looks towards the doorway, where* **Colin** *will come through with news of her fate.*

Blackout.

Scene Two

Five hours later. The quiet before the storm.

Barbara *in the room; we can see her through the door in the light from the window.* **Adnan** *revealed on stage. He is watching a film on his phone, the final scene of* Billy Elliot *dubbed into Arabic.*

Emma *enters – she goes to wash up her mugs.*

Adnan   Billy. It's *Billy Elliot.*

They smile at each other.

Something kind passes between them. **Emma** *is about to speak to him.*

Tharwa *enters.*

Tharwa   I need to say something. The cup is yours. I just confused

Emma   Yeah it is

Tharwa   I didn't mean to make you stress. I'm really sorry for your baby

Emma   Umm. It's ok

Tharwa   I am also a mother, madam. My children are joining me soon

Emma   Yeah – oh great.

Well thank you

She goes back to the room. **Adnan** *and* **Tharwa** *alone.*

Adnan   Everything is ok?

Pause.

Tharwa   Yes. excuse me, where are you from?

Adnan   Syria

Tharwa   Do you speak Arabic?

Adnan   Yes. My name is Adnan

He stands up and places his hand on his chest, in the formal Arab style. She offers her hand for a handshake.

The following is all in Arabic.

Tharwa   Hello, my brother, I'm from Sudan

They shake hands.

Adnan   Hello and welcome /

Tharwa   How are you /

Adnan   I'm fine /

Tharwa   Let me offer you tea

Adnan   I have juice. Can I offer you some?

He crosses to get cups. She hesitates then sits. Silence as he brings cups. As he places cups.

Tharwa   No, thank you. In Sudan we drink this *fresh* from the tree, not from these cartons

Adnan   But this is good actually!

Tharwa   In Sudan we have mangos, lemons, all growing around /

Adnan   *Mashallah* (God willed it)

Pause.

Tharwa   Did you hurt your foot?

Adnan   No, no, everything is ok

Tharwa   In Sudan we say Syria is beautiful, we say Syria is beautiful /

Adnan   Yes . . .

Tharwa   It will get better *Inshallah* (God willing)

Adnan   *Inshallah*

Tharwa   *Inshallah*

Pause.

In Sudan we just love Syrian soap operas!

Adnan   Oh really?

Tharwa   We really love Mohanned and . . .

Adnan   Not 'Mohanned and Noor'?!

Tharwa   Yes 'Mohanned and Noor', exactly! Honestly I love it! I watched it all the time with my family. Honestly we loved it.

Adnan   But 'Mohanned and Noor' is actually Turkish

Tharwa   Oh really?!

She laughs and covers her smile with her scarf.

Adnan   Yes, it's only dubbed into Syrian Arabic /

Tharwa   It's really Turkish? I really thought it was Syrian

Paige *enters and goes to the fridge. She runs back to the room.*

Tharwa   That little girl is beautiful!

Adnan   Yes . . . What's the name of the woman in that room?

Tharwa   Emma, her name is Emma, she lives with those children, they are nice actually. But the guy in that room, I don't like him he scares me.

Pause.

But *Elhamdullah* (Thank God)

Long silence where she thinks about her own family.

Elhamdullah

Silence.

Adnan   I'm happy to have met you

Tharwa   Me too

He gets up to go.

Take care of yourself

Adnan   Yes

Tharwa   Take care of yourself

Adnan   And you, goodbye

Tharwa   Goodbye

They end the conversation. **Adnan** *leaves.* **Tharwa** *is left alone again in the common room.*

Tree hits skylight.

Barbara *enters.*

Barbara   I like to look at that tree

Yeh

We had one like that at home

I want to take Colin back to the sea, where I was brought up.

Tharwa   I miss the river Nile too.

Paige *goes to the bathroom.* **Emma** *follows after with a toilet roll.*

Tharwa *smiles.*

Enter **Colin**.

Barbara   How did it go?

Colin   Fine yeh.

Barbara   Did you show her the letter

Colin   Yeah

Barbara   How long? One week two weeks?

Colin   There's no housing.

Barbara   But did you give them the doctor's letter . . .

Colin   Made no difference, Mum

Barbara   But

She sits.

Colin   .

Barbara (*barely audible*)   Maybe I should go back to that home and die

Colin   What?

Barbara   I just thought we could've moved back to the coast

Colin   Mom, stop talking about the seaside, we only went there once

Pause.

Barbara   A cup of tea?

Colin   No fuck it

Emma *and* **Paige** *leave the bathroom and go into their bedroom.*

Colin   There's nothing for us, Mum. I was there five hours, she only gave me five minutes. Sat behind a piece of glass. She said they haven't got anything, they're still assessing our case . . .

Barbara   And?

Colin   She upset me, Mum.

I got upset with her.

He goes to the room.

Emma *enters.*

Barbara *waits.*

Emma   You ok?

Barbara   Yeh

Enter **Adnan**.

Adnan   You're a student? Hi

Emma   Hi. Yeh. Trying to be

Adnan   What?

Emma   It's massage and wellness therapy. What about you?

Adnan   Yes, I was a primary school teacher

Enter **Dean** *carrying large shopping bags that seem used already.*

Emma   Dean, when did you go shopping?

Paige *runs to* **Dean**, **Jason** *follows. They attack the shopping bags.*

Dean   Hold on, hold on, wait for dinner will you

Paige   Is there anything I can eat now? I'm hungry

She picks out a pack of mince pies.

These?

Dean   No, we're going to save those for Christmas

Paige   But I'm hungry

Dean   Here you go

He gives her a packet of cornflakes. **Jason** *pulls out a packet of biscuits.*

Dean   Don't just eat the biscuits, take them to the room

Jason *takes the two bags into the bedroom.*

Emma   You only got tinned vegetables?

Dean   I had to go to the food bank.

Emma   But I thought you said we'd be fine you were /
seeing them today to sort it out

Dean   I know but it's what I had to do.

They've cut our money for a while. And we have to stay here
till they start it up again.

Emma   But we've done nothing wrong – they're just
punishing /

Dean   I know, Emma – I'm going back there tomorrow.

Silence. **Emma** *goes towards the kitchen.*

Paige   Is everything ok, Dad?

Dean   Everything's fine, babe. Don't worry about
anything ok?

Emma *begins to heat up some soup.*

Dean *opens his backpack and pulls out some Christmas decorations.*

Dean   Hey, look what I got for Christmas

Paige   Cool

Dean   Yeah? Do you want to come and help me put them up?

Paige   Yeah

Dean   Come on then. Where shall we put it?

Paige   Up high

They do so with some excitement and then it fades to something simpler. The cold returns.

Dean (*to* **Jason**)   You going to help?

Jason   I'm really tired

Dean   We're going to eat soon

Pause.

Why don't you do this one, Jase?

Jason   .

He does.

Dean   Paige

Paige

I'm sorry I shouted, Paige

Paige   It's ok, Dad

Dean   I promise when we sort this out I'll take you to McDonald's

Or Burger King

Paige   McDonald's

Dean   You deserve it

What'll you have?

Paige   I'll have a Happy Meal and some nuggets

Dean   Yeah?

Paige   And ketchup and

Chips

Dean   Whatever you want

Paige   When are we going to get a house, Dad?

Dean   Soon, promise

Right, come on, mate

Jason *comes over.*

Emma *pours the soup into bowls.*

Dean   Thank you, Emma

They eat in silence.

A long silence. Just the sound of the family eating soup.

Paige *looks over at the Christmas decorations.*

Paige   Are we going to be here for Christmas, Dad?

Pause. **Barbara** *wanders over to the sink. Takes a tablet with a glass of water.*

Jason   Thanks

He exits to the room.

Paige   I'm still hungry

Dean   Do you want some more soup?

Paige   I want pudding

Barbara   I've got something for you

Dean   No, you're alright

Paige   I want it

Dean   No, Paige

Barbara   I'll get it.

Dean   No, honestly it's ok

Barbara *exits. He clears the table.*

Dean   Come to the room?

Emma   .

Dean *goes to the room.*

Dean   Em?

Emma   Yeh coming

You going to get ready for bed, Paige?

She goes into the room, leaving **Paige** *alone. She turns the lights off.*

Paige *sits alone, in silence, for a short while.*

The sound of the tree on the roof. She wanders towards the tree in the darkness and then stands under the skylight. Suddenly a drop of water falls from the roof and hits her. She jumps back in alarm but then slowly comes forward again and collects the raindrops falling through the roof into her outstretched palms.

Blackout.

Act Three

Scene One

Some days later, but not many. The day of the school nativity.

Lights up on **Jason** *sitting outside the bedroom with iPad on. After a time,* **Paige** *enters practising 'Away in a Manger'.*

Jason   What the fuck are you doing?

Paige   Practising.

You need to practise too, Jason

Jason   No

Paige   You have to, you promised you'd do it.

Jason   I'm not doing it

Paige   I'll get your costume?

Jason   I don't want a costume

Paige   Say your lines?

She gives a piece of paper to him.

Say them, Jason

Jason   First Shepherd. 'And there were shepherds living out in the fields nearby' /

Paige   Do it properly, Jason

Jason   'keeping watch over their flocks at night. An angel of the Lord appeared to them and they were terrified' /

Paige   / terrified

(*Sings.*) Away in a manger, no crib for a bed . . .

Jason *puts music on the iPad.*

Paige   Jason, turn that off. Jason. Jason, stop it

Fuck you, Jason

She gives up and goes to the bedroom in a huff.

Barbara *emerges.* **Jason** *turns off the music.* **Barbara** *goes to the sink but then changes direction and stops in the middle of the room.*

She defecates on the floor. **Jason** *sits silently. She keeps walking to the toilet. There is a puddle of faeces on the floor.*

At the toilet door:

Barbara   Col! Col!

Colin *emerges and goes to help her.*

Jason *goes to the kitchen.*

Barbara   I'm sorry I'm sorry I'm sorry. (*Cries.*)

Jason *knocks at the door.*

Jason   Emma! Emma!

The old woman shat on the floor

Emma   Excuse me!

Colin *and* **Barbara** *ignore her.*

They talk in the toilet, inaudible, sounds of him getting her changed and cleaned.

Barbara *is crying.*

Emma   My kids wanna play out here do you just wanna clean it up

Please! Please just

Excuse me

FUCK

She gets cleaning stuff and starts cleaning.

Barbara *comes out,* **Paige** *comes out.*

Paige   Ugh ugh sick

Barbara   Fuck off! FUCK OFF

Paige *goes back into the bedroom.*

Emma   Is that my dressing gown?

Colin   Sorry it was hanging behind the door. I . . .

Emma   I don't fucking want it now you can keep it

Long pause. As he's out of room she goes to pick up the bin and returns to cleaning.

He emerges with the dressing gown and gives it to her– it dangles over the faeces, and accidentally some gets on it.

Emma   Did you just put my fucking dressing gown in the shit.

Colin   . . .

Emma   Are you mental /

Colin   Sorry I'm sorry like it's yours I just wanted to /

Emma (*as she pushes him back to the room*)   I told you I didn't want it. She has shat all over the fucking floor. Does it look clean to you, mate. You can fucking keep it. Give it to your fucking mum.

She slaps him in the face.

Pause – like she's seen herself.

Colin *breaks down.*

Colin   Please don't hit me.

He exits.

Emma *cleans up, putting the dressing gown in the bin bag. It takes a period of time and she's nearly vomiting as she does it. She goes to put the bin bag outside.*

Colin *emerges to apologise.* **Emma** *returns.*

Emma   I'm so sorry, I'm sorry, I'm so so sorry, I'm sorry

Colin   Can I touch it?

Emma   Sorry?

Colin   The baby

Emma   No . . . I . . .

Colin   Please

He slowly moves towards her.

Emma   Careful

He touches her belly. They look at each other. Slowly they begin to smile. He cries.

Silence.

Barbara *calls from the bedroom then enters.*

Barbara   Col?

Col?

Colin

I need to speak to you

Colin   Not now please

Barbara   It's important, love

Colin   Not now, Mum

Barbara   I just need to speak to you /

Colin   Just leave me alone, Mum

Dean *enters and crosses past* **Barbara** *and* **Colin** *to the bedroom.*

Barbara   Col

Colin   Just leave it.

I've wiped your fucking arse for you, what more do you want?

Sorry

He exits.

Barbara (*calling after him*)   I love you

Dean *goes into the room*

Dean   What's going on?

Jason   Dad, the old lady shat on the floor and Emma had to clean it up

Barbara *goes towards her room.*

Barbara   Do forgive me.

I don't know what I'm doing

She exits. **Emma** *goes to the bedroom door. She stops and sits outside the room.*

Dean *enters.* **Emma** *moves to the table.*

Dean   Em, Jason told me what happened. I'm sorry /

Emma *gets up. Moves away from his touch.*

Pause. **Dean** *goes to the bedroom door.*

Emma   I love you, Dean

I just don't know who is going to help us

Dean   I'm trying my best

Emma   Dean. Come here

Dean *goes to* **Emma**

Emma   Are we going to be ok?

They hug and kiss.

Dean   I love you.

Paige *comes in. She is dressed in an angel costume ready for her nativity play.*

Barbara *enters.* **Adnan** *enters with his bags.*

Paige   Dad, Dad, look at my costume

Dean   You look beautiful

He and **Emma** *go towards the bedroom.*

Dean   Oh, you're off are you?

Adnan   Yes

Dean   Good luck then

The family exit to their bedroom.

Adnan *crosses to exit.*

Barbara   Bye

Adnan   Bye

Adnan *exits.*

Silence.

Colin *comes back. He goes towards* **Barbara**.

Colin   I'm sorry, Mum

Barbara   You'll be alright when I'm gone

When I'm gone you'll be dancing

Colin   I'll have a fucking party

Barbara   You'll get a job maybe, find a girl

Pause.

Col, I'm going to die

Colin   We're all going to fucking die

They laugh.

As he walks back to the room, barely audible:

Love you Mum

He exits.

Pause.

Enter **Paige**, **Jason**, **Dean** *and* **Emma**.

Barbara   Goodbye, little angel

Paige.   I've got my costume

The family exit, **Dean** *trailing behind.*

Barbara   Could I have a glass of water

Dean   Yeh

Barbara   Do you like water?

Dean   Do I like water? I have to like water

Barbara   Do you like swimming in the sea

Dean   I haven't been for a while

Barbara   I like water. I used to swim in the sea and my dad would say look, look, Barbara!

Dean *is desperate to get away.*

Dean   Right yeh

Barbara   Gorgeous

Dean   What?

Barbara   I'm very sorry about what happened earlier

Dean   Yeah well they're only little so it can't really happen again

Barbara   I love being in water. Not like here

I love Colin as much as the sea, as big as the sea. (*Laughs.*)

Dean   What?

Barbara   NOT LIKE 'ERE!

Silence.

Fucking Floyd Mattison

I went to the sea once, I was running towards the sea and my dad he said oh look at Barbara go, and I jumped in and I was /

Dean   Yeh /

Barbara   swimming and I could see everyone looking at me . . . /

Dean   Yeh sorry I better

Barbara   Love?

Dean   .

He's gone.

The tree hits the roof.

Barbara *gets up. She leaves her stick.*

She walks towards the audience, she is very frail.

She sees them; looks at them straight in the face.

She uses the audience to support her as she walks out of the theatre.

Silence.

Tharwa *enters and makes a call in Arabic. Her young daughter answers.*

Tharwa   Tala, Tala, Mumma loves you.

Do you remember when I used to sing to you, doha doha?

She sings her a lullaby.

Suddenly, mid-verse: Blackout.

www.ingramcontent.com/pod-product-compliance
Ingram Content Group UK Ltd.
Pitfield, Milton Keynes, MK11 3LW, UK
UKHW020708280225
455688UK00012B/322